micro space global time an architectural manifesto

micro spaces for global living and working, responding to the interrelations of old and new spatialities and temporalities; physical, electronic and mental spaces that reflect the social change engineered and predicted by the digital revolution; spatial conglomerates implementing and allowing new forms of communication, relaxation, socializing and pleasure.

Micro Space/Global Time: An Architectural Manifesto
at the MAK Center for Art and Architecture, L. A., Schindler House
Exhibition dates: 2 June – 11 July 1999

at the MAK, Vienna
Exhibition dates: 2 June – 11 July 1999

The exhibition presents the 8 digital prints comprising the Micro Space/Global Time Portfolio published by Muse [X] Editions in a limited edition of 20 and 10 artists proofs, individually signed and numbered.

Exhibition and Publication: Blythe Alison-Mayne, Daniela Zyman
Program Coordination: LouAnne Greenwald; Assistance: Stefan Zucker

Special thanks to: Friends of the Schindler House, MAK Governing Committee and Muse [X] Editions (Los Angeles) especially: Jane Hart, Director; Randy Green, Owner; Astrid Giese Wright, Project Coordinator; and printers: Kevin Pontutti, James Cherry and Adam Williams.

Graphic Design and Portfolio: Catherine Lorenz, Los Angeles

MAK Center for Art and Architecture, L. A.
Schindler House, 835 North Kings Road, West Hollywood, California 90069
tel (323) 651-1510 fax (323) 651-2340 email MAKcenter@earthlink.net

MAK Artists and Architects in Residence Program
Pearl M. Mackey House
1137-1141 South Cochran Avenue, Los Angeles, California 90019

MAK – Austrian Museum of Applied Arts
Stubenring 5, 1010 Vienna, Austria
tel (431) 71136-0 fax (431) 713 1026 email office@MAK.at

ISBN 0-9671862-1-8

MAK Center for Art and Architecture L. A.

micro space global time an architectural manifesto

Vito Acconci/Acconci Studio, New York
Neil M. Denari/Neil M. Denari Architects, Los Angeles
Craig Hodgetts and Hsin-Ming Fung/Hodgetts + Fung Design Associates, Los Angeles
Greg Lynn/FORM, Los Angeles
Thom Mayne/Morphosis, Los Angeles
Eric Owen Moss/Eric Owen Moss Architects, Los Angeles
Wolf D. Prix, Helmut Swiczinsky/COOP HIMMELB(L)AU, Vienna
Andrea Zittel and Jonathan Williams, Los Angeles

Edited by Peter Noever for the MAK Center for Art and Architecture, L. A. and
MAK – Austrian Museum of Applied Arts, Vienna

on today's architecture

Peter Noever

The infinite space of the Internet challenges our concepts of continuous temporality and spatiality as well as our notions of the public and the private. Both the site and function of architecture seem to have changed, thus provoking the question: How has the digital revolution affected architectural space?

One of the tasks most relevant to architecture, the organization and design of urban space with respect to the increasing movement of people into and out of city centers, is taking a new direction due to the worldwide intervention of new media. The data highway, now an almost archaic architectural metaphor, has reversed urban spatial structures: fewer people leave their living space to go to work – work comes to them in the form of digital data. The microcosm of the individual desk at home replaces the open-plan office: overloaded networks resemble commuter traffic jams.

Gradually, the World Wide Web spins itself into today's world and creates an immense diversity of spaces and spatial concepts. One of the tasks of today's architecture is the redefinition of the transformed places and structures of social life; if microcosm and macrocosm, the virtual and the real continue to permeate each other increasingly, cyberspace becomes an additional architectural space (of agitation). Considering these conditions, the architectural response is necessarily both concrete and utopian: concrete because it must respond to the present context, and utopian because conditions are constantly shifting in a way that is difficult to anticipate. The digital revolution transforms real space through a mutual adaptation, impacting everything from the ergonomic demands for workstations to the simulation of globally operative urban landscapes that need to be newly established.

Micro Space/Global Time: An Architectural Manifesto, published by the MAK Center, L. A. in cooperation with Muse [X] Editions is positioned in this field of tension between microcosm and macrocosm. The images reflect the restructuring of the function of architecture in response to the changing concept of space as it is effected by digitalization. Eight contemporary artists and architects or teams articulate their outlooks on various aspects of this issue. The participants were asked to create "a microenvironment for global living and working which responds to the current (and future) possibility of living and working in a single site." Their responses focus on both linking the real body to the virtual world by means of electronic implants and the need to create places of isolation and freedom despite the possibility of constant connection. They have devised architectural systems whose elements are interconnected in such a manner that a change in any one field affects the entire structure. The images of the Micro Space/Global Time prints portfolio have been generated with elaborate design programs and printed with the most advanced digital techniques – images of a world inscribed relentlessly into real space.

This project would not have been possible without the exemplary engagement and support of the artists and architects who accepted and surpassed the digital challenge and envisioned new physical, mental and electronic spaces and environments for heterogeneous forms of life and Muse [X] Editions, especially Jane Hart who initiated this proposal. I extend my sincere gratitude to all those involved.

revisiting the edge

Saskia Sassen

When I was asked by the MAK Center, L. A. to respond to the Architectural Manifesto on Micro Space/Global Time I had difficulty imagining how my work on macroenvironments could be engaged by micro-environments. I had not thought about the possibility that such "microenvironments for living and working" might also constitute such a site – one where the juxtapositions of different spatialities and temporalities are thick, charged. While I was not asked to discuss the projects presented by the participating architects and artists, I found them extremely compelling and helpful in thinking through some of the issues. Notwithstanding the different vocabularies and organizing questions, I recognized certain intellectual resonances with my concerns, some of which I allude to in the following text. Several of the images, in my reading, pivot on this strategic juxtaposition of different spatialities and temporalities, even though at some levels they may represent themselves as belonging exclusively to the new digital world.

The experience of the global digital era is partial. It is not an all-encompassing umbrella. The multiple processes that constitute it inhabit and shape specific, rather than universal structurations of the economic, the political, the cultural, the subjective. In so doing, new spatialities and temporalities are produced, co-existing yet distinct from the master temporality and spatiality of the "national" and of spatial hierarchies based on size which have dominated for a century. In the interplay of their difference, strategic openings have emerged.

The sites that concern me represent variants of strategic juxtapositions among different temporal and spatial orders.[1] These sites can be made to work analytically and to help us understand larger, more elusive dynamics. For instance, I would argue that we exist today in the play between two master temporalities: one of these is a collapsing temporality – that of the national state as a historic institution, a master temporality often thought of as historic time. The other is a new temporality, that of the global digital era. We do not exist exclusively in one or the other. Further, we operate in a topography that weaves between actual and digital space. There is no purely virtual company or human, even as we are increasingly relocating activities to digital spaces and locating digital capacities in the human body. The intersection of actual and digital space is unwittingly, perhaps, thought of as a line that divides two mutually exclusive zones. I propose to open up this line into an "analytic borderland" which demands its own empirical specification and theorization, and contains its own possibilities for various types of practices – from architectural to rhetorical. The space of the computer screen, which one might posit as a version of the intersection, will not do, or is at most a partial enactment of this intersection.

Three points come to mind in the particular case of the Micro Space/Global Time project:

First, global cities and the microenvironments presented here each structure a zone that spans the globe but it is a zone embedded in, juxtaposed with older temporalities and spatialities. The new interface economies which dominate the global city, are produced, precisely by this juxtaposition. I would posit that the microenvironments considered here have a similar dynamic. They present themselves as self-contained settings made possible by digital capacities. Yet don't they arise precisely out of the fact of the limitations of the non-digital condition? Financial capital illustrates the more general point I am trying to make: its ascendance and capacity to subject other forms of capital to its modes has to do with the different temporality (much shorter than that of other forms of capital) and spatiality (hypermobility due to its dematerialized outputs). How would this work in an analysis of the microenvironments we are concerned with here? It seems to me that the design presented by the Acconci Studio captures a dynamic of juxtaposition between different spatialities and temporalities: their proposed "prosthetic skeleton" exists partly as a function of the body and gains its ascendance through its superior flexibility/mobility.

Second, understanding the new spatialities, notably that of economic globalization, only in terms of hypermobility and space/time compression – the dominant markers in today's conceptualization – is inadequate. Hypermobility and space/time compression need to be produced, and this requires vast concentrations of material and not such mobile facilities and infrastructures. Microenvironments for "global living and working" are subject to the same tension between global span and sited materialities. Here I find an interesting conceptual resonance with Eric Owen Moss' wall-building project in his effort to negotiate the relationship between the limitless freedom of the wall, so to speak, and the enormous amount of drawings, as well as the metal and stone work that went into making it. It revisits the tension between that which is experienced as limitless, dematerialized capacity, as in the digital, and the materialities that are sited.

Thirdly, while spanning the globe, the new zone that is being structured is inhabited/constituted by multiple units or locals – it is not only a flow of transactions or one large encompassing system. The global city is a function of a global network – there is no such thing as a single global city as you might have had with the empires of the past, each with its capital. The microenvironments called for in this project by the MAK Center are similarly meant to be part of global networks. In the case of my research, this means that we need to decode what is local (or national?) in such locals; what is local amidst that which has historically been constructed as local because it is sited in a place. Further, we must specify what are the new territorial and institutional conditionalities of the local – of that which is present in a place – in a global digital era.

All three of these features raise a question about how the edge works, about the presence or absence of intersections between different environments, about what happens to contextuality.

A macroenvironment such as the global city or the types of microenvironments presented in this exhibition, operating partly in actual space and partly in globe-spanning digital space, cannot easily be contextualized in terms of their surroundings. The orientation is simultaneously towards itself and towards the global. The intensity of each environment's internal transactions is such that it overrides all considerations of the broader locality or region within which it exists. On a larger scale, I find that global cities develop a stronger orientation towards global markets and towards each other than to their hinterlands, thereby overriding a key proposition in the urban systems literature, to wit – that cities and urban systems integrate and articulate national territory.[2] Further, as COOP HIMMELB(L)AU argue, "the coincidence of systems – both as built space and as media space – becomes the basis for new designs and projects," further contributing to the intensity of an environment's internal transactions.

What then is the "context," the local, here? The new networked subeconomy of the global city occupies a strategic, partly deterritorialized geography that cuts across borders and connects a variety of points on the globe. It occupies only a fraction of its "local" setting. Its boundaries are not those of the city where it is partly located, nor those of the "neighborhood." This subeconomy interfaces both its vast concentration of the very material resources needed when it hits the ground and its global span or cross-border geography. Its interlocutor is not the surrounding, the context, but its global scope.

What this tearing away of the context and its replacement with the global dimension could mean for architecture generally, and the particular Architectural Manifesto of this exhibition, is yet unclear. The strategic operation is not the search for a connection with the "surroundings," the context; it is, rather, its installation in a strategic cross-border geography constituted through multiple "locals." Rescalings are a fundamental dynamic today in a global digital system. In the case of the economy I see a rescaling of old spatial hierarchies: local, regional, national, global – this conventional hierarchy no longer holds. Going to the next scale in terms of size is no longer how integration is achieved. The local now transacts directly with the global – the global installs itself in locals and the global is itself constituted through a multiplicity of locals.[3]

Architecturally, there are many possible negotiations of these issues. Greg Lynn's *Embryological Space* is a radical negotiation, insofar as not only all of the 2,048 panels in each object, but also the "ground" is internally networked. A "deformation in the object has a corresponding effect on the field around it." The internal intensity of transactions is such that the surrounding ceases to matter. Similarly, Andrea Zittel and Jonathan Williams explore "what it would feel like to be alone in the middle of a vast ocean" using computer generated environments to do so. Both of these projects neutralize the question of the edge by relocating the center of intensity inside the microenvironment through a complex set of operations: an installation of capacities that make possible a multiplication of internal transactions. Juxtaposition with that which it is not, ceases to matter.

The multiplication of internal transactions can indeed constitute environments, as is the case partly in global finance, but the capacity to do so is predicated on juxtapositions. Analytically and operationally this new world of business activities – the networked subeconomy that dominates global cities – is a sort of borderzone, it does not belong to either of the two or more sectors among which it negotiates its own existence and sources for profit.

I have used the notion of "analytic borderlands" to open up the line that is represented or experienced as dividing two mutually exclusive zones – to open up that line into a borderzone that demands its own theorization and empirical specification and that can accommodate its own distinct practices. The global city is one instantiation on a rather macrolevel.[4] Other microenvironments presented in this exhibition also operate on this borderzone pivoting on the juxtaposition of different spatialities and temporalities. Neil Denari and Roberto Davolio's three diagrams of conceptual continuously curving sections, each representing space as it is hybridized over a 24 hour length of time operates precisely on this juxtaposition. Craig Hodgetts' and Hsin-Ming Fung's microarchitecture, *RE.T.V.* – a device to be implanted in the cornea of the human eye allowing one to modify what he/she is seeing – is a way of negotiating spatiality through the context or its absence. Thom Mayne's project is centered in such a borderzone. It reminds me of my perception of the global city – new spatialities and temporalities embedded in and filtered through older ones. This continually shifting overlay of old and new, actual and digital, local and global blurs the lines which once defined the edges of their respective zones. Hence, a complex task of decoding is necessary to understand this landscape, if you must.

Saskia Sassen is Professor of Sociology, The University of Chicago and Centennial Visiting Professor, The London School of Economics. Her most recent books are Globalization and its Discontents *(New York: New Press 1998) and* Losing Control? Sovereignty in an Age of Globalization*. (Columbia University Press, 1996). Her books have been translated into ten languages.*

NOTES

1 I develop this at greater length in "The De-Nationalization of Time and Space." (*Public Culture*, Millennium Issue on Globalization, 2000).

2 This may have been the case during the period when mass manufacturing and mass consumption were the dominant growth machines in developed economies and thrived on the possibility of a national scale. But it is not today with the ascendance of digitalized, globalized, dematerialized sectors such as finance.

3 I also see this in the political realm, particularly the kind of "global" politics attributed to the Internet. I think of it rather as a multiplicity of localized operations, but with a difference: they are part of the global network that is the Internet. This produces a "knowing" that re-marks the local. (See the chapter "Electronic Space and Power", *Globalization and its Discontents*. New York: New Press, 1998)

4 The work I am doing currently on the state is another "analytic borderland," implicated by incipiently denationalized (highly specialized) institutional orders that negotiate between a) the world of the exclusive sovereign authority of national states over their national territories and b) the implantation of global operations in those same territories. (*Losing Control? Sovereignty in an Age of Globalization*. New York: Columbia University Press, 1996)

Vito Acconci/Acconci Studio
Vito Acconci, Luis Vera, Dario Nunez, Azarakhsh Damood, Thomas King

World in your Bones

The under structure of this microenvironment is screwed into your bones, like a prosthetic skeleton. It lives on your back, on your limbs, on your head; it moves as you move, you barely notice it as you go about your business. When you feel some need, the plot thickens: the tubes slide, pivot, telescope out – you become your own chair, your own bed, your own vehicle. A micro-shell fans out, over your head: your head becomes your office. A macro-shell fans out, over your body: your body becomes your house. Visitors enter your house, as if coming in under your clothes. Your house leeches onto a building: you own your own apartment, you move your apartment from building to building. Your house leeches onto a plane, a train, a ship, a car: you ride for free. (You don't have this tool in your hands yet, let alone in your body; right now it's all on paper, staring you in the face like a dare; you shuffle the page around, you can read it from any direction.)

There's a world out there: grab it as it goes by...
You take your apartment with you

Neil Denari and Roberto Davolio
Neil M. Denari Architects

What to do?

What hasn't already been said about the great inverted discourse of our time, about the shrinking of the world's space and natural resources in direct opposition to the exponentially expanding digital spaces of the global computer network being constructed around us? Had not the ground plowed in the 1960's through projects like Michael Webb's Cushicle (the imploded) and Kenzo Tange's Tokyo Bay expansion (the exploded) given us the definitive statements on scale, technology, and proximity? And what about Neil Armstrong, should he be forgotten as a maker of new space? After all, from capsules to lunar deserts, he knows the scale shifts at work in the questions posed by the MAK Center project probably better than any architect. More recently, Paul Virilio's writings have produced a new outlook on the inverted cones of miniaturization and proliferation. There has never been a more poetic and indeed overwhelmingly fatalistic view of the effects of speed, ecological traumas, the birth of placelessness, and the continuing loss of presence. Virilio's position, somewhere between hysteria and true lament, covers the emotional gamut at the end of this century.

Why do it?

With the whole panoply of ideas about the debilitating and enabling aspects of contemporary technology as a backdrop, our proposal has become a modest one, a diagrammatic one, a search for an idea between here and there, and indeed, between here and now. It could only become an idea about time and place, not a place in time.

How to do it?

Three conceptual, continuously curving sections are diagrammed, each one about "the deflection of the normative". An automobile, HVAC, and a swimming pool are movement conditions which deform the extruded envelopes of a series of conceptual living and working spaces. These extrusions are then hybridized across a 24-hour length of time. The dimension of each hour is not determined to be specific, only relative. So, with time as a specific element, and dimension as a vague element, this project attempts to display time as the most meaningful commodity, an absolute a priori to space. Each hybrid extrusion is then effected laterally through the forces of movement in the envelope. The resulting geometry is a wire-frame that becomes a kind of vague structuring device for the evanescent envelope surrounding it.

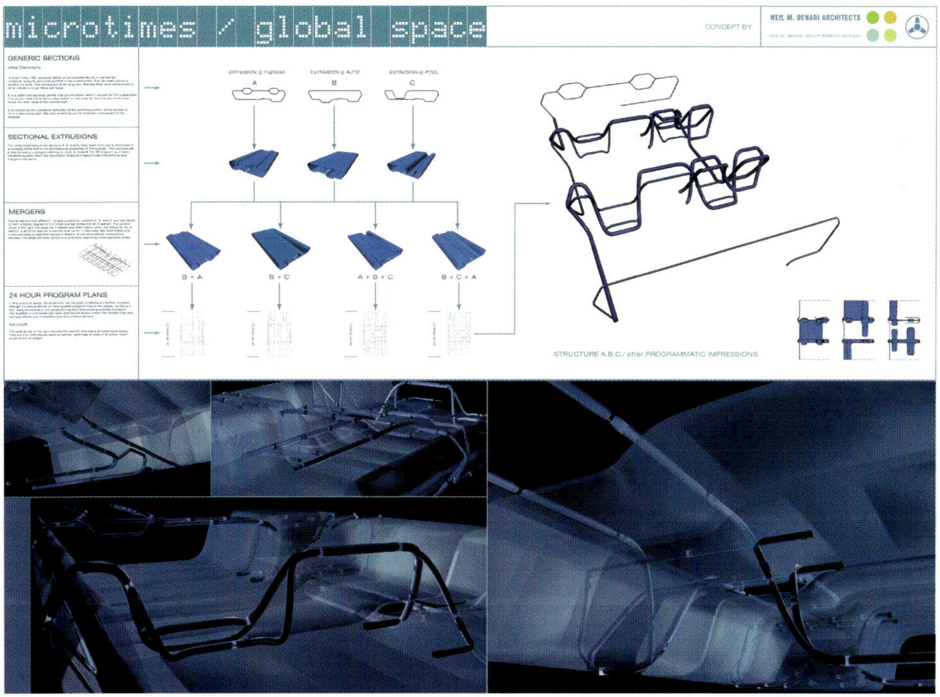

Printed in the USA by MUSE | X | EDITIONS, Los Angeles

Craig Hodgetts and Hsin-Ming Fung
Hodgetts + Fung Design Associates

RE.T.V.

If by seeing we negotiate the world about us, could we extend the environment to the virtual by means of an architecture which modifies "what we are seeing", rather than "what we see"? Such an architecture could discard the physical constraints of an external reality and achieve its effects by producing an image directly on the retina. Perhaps it may even be possible to toggle between such a virtual image and the enveloping image of "reality", or create an illuminated version of reality to inhabit a designated work environment, the user would be free to apply his/her skills in any settings desired – even the bath!

RE.T.V. explores the micro architecture of a device designed for direct implantation in the cornea of the human eye. Founded on an annular integrated circuit with F.M. multi-plexing and high resolution image processing, the device draws power from an immersible bimetallic anode-cathode array within the amniotic fluid of the eye itself, and is thus capable of maintenance-free operation for the life of the wearer.

Imaging is accomplished by a pixelated lens array at the site of the cornea, acting much like a conventional corneal transplant, but for its ability to superimpose synthesized images directly on those produced by the surrounding reality, or to replace them altogether by the activation of a translucent lamination composed of a liquid crystal membrane.

It has been possible to reduce the bulk of the device by eliminating on-board memory and math-processing functions in favor of a unique knuckle-control module to be worn on the hand, which controls both the implanted Micro E.V. and a belt-mounted base unit by means of a dedicated F.M. transceiver.

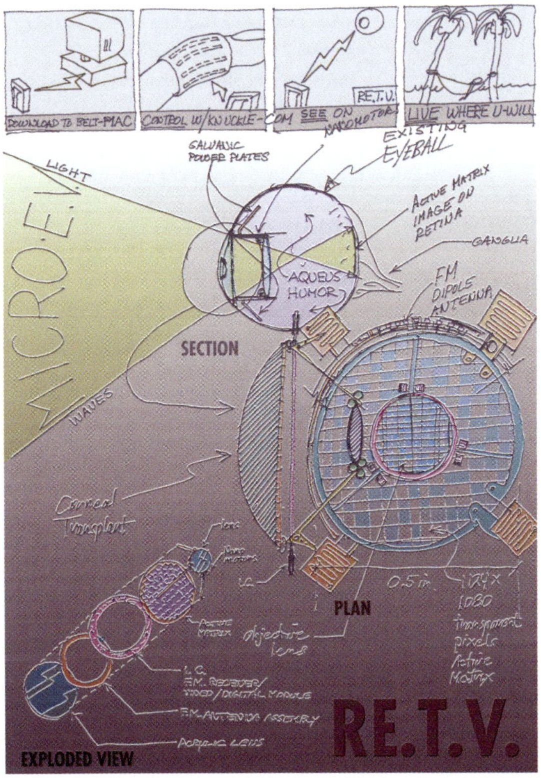
DOWNLOAD TO BELT-MAC
CONTROL W/KNUCKLE-COM
SEE ON NANOMOTOR
RE.T.V.
LIVE WHERE U-WILL
EXISTING EYEBALL
GALVANIC POWER PLATES
LIGHT
MICRO.E.V.
WAVES
Active MATRIX IMAGE ON RETINA
GANGLIA
AQUEUS HUMOR
FM DIPOLS ANTENNA
SECTION
Corneal Transplant
PLAN
0.5 in.
objective lens
EXPLODED VIEW
RE.T.V.

Greg Lynn

FORM

Embryological Space

In the history of Modern architecture, with special regard to housing, building has been conceived as an assembly of independent parts, or a kit. In this study, space is enclosed in a surface composed of over 2,048 panels, all of which are unique in their shape and size. These panels are networked so that a change in any individual panel is transmitted throughout every other panel in the whole. A set of controlling points is organized across this surface so that groups of these generic panels can be effected to bud into more specific forms or "nodules". In every instance of this surface, there is a constant number of panels with a consistent relationship to their neighboring panels. No element is ever added or subtracted.

The volume is defined as a soft flexible surface of curves rather than as a fixed set of rigid points. Instead of cutting windows and door openings into the surface, an alternative strategy of torn, shredded and louvered openings were invented allowing for openings that respected the soft geometry of the curved envelopes. The surface envelopes are connected with a landscape so that any alteration in the object is transmitted onto a ground surface. Thereby a deformation in the volume has a corresponding effect on the field around it, facilitating openings, views and circulation on a potential site.

The curved chips of the envelope are made of wood, polymers and steel all of which are fabricated with robotic computer-controlled milling and high-pressure, water-jet cutting machinery.

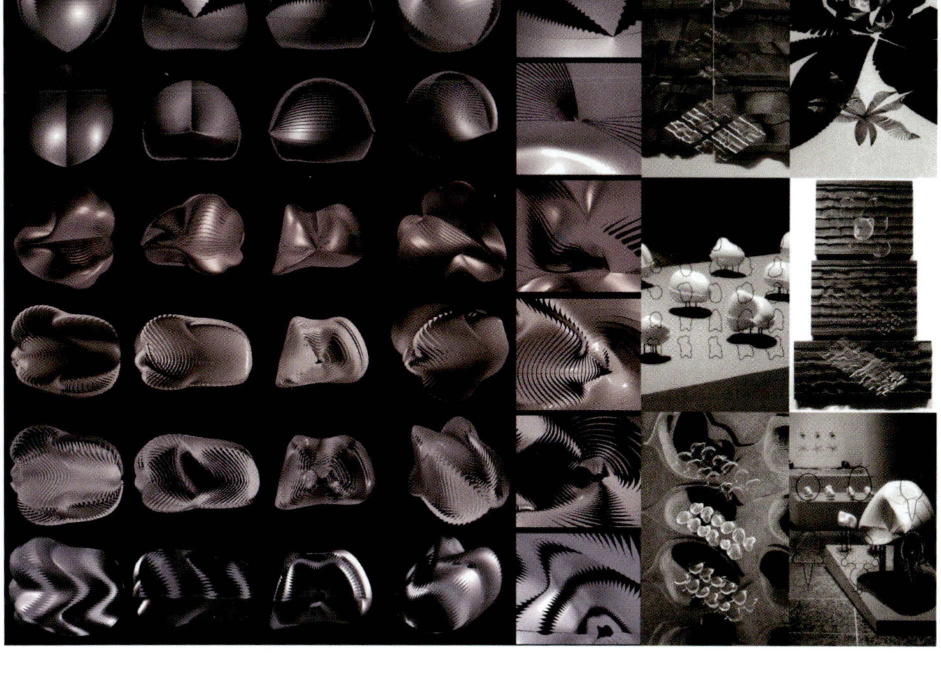

Thom Mayne

Morphosis

This is a full-size city. There is a possibility to live and work, both digital and real (practically equal). You don't need to go anywhere, it's an ordinary spot, yet nothing is familiar (maybe the volcano). You'll find all the necessities... relaxation, socializing, pleasure in all possible combinations at top speed (don't be afraid). No two things look alike, things with things (not the easiest solution). An upside down pyramid (single site). A churchy zone (to be repaired, outsides have settled in their places). A 24-hour chat room (nobody knows whether it is straight or curved, a slightly crooked space). The official district (reality – raucous, gaudy, hooting). Unchartered territory. A bar at the corner (a locked room). A place for you.

One slip of the tongue and it could backfire (here be monsters), a dream which was later forgotten, a wasteland (absolute visual neutrality), where knowledge ends and darkness begins.

Eric Owen Moss
Eric Owen Moss Architects

It's about a tiny project – a wall, actually, about 30' x 30' – but one of the most complicated constructions I've completed.

The essential question is the apparently contradictory relationship between an idea of architectural freedom and the drawing control needed to deliver it.

The wall, in a conceptual sense, is freedom itself – limitless. But the kind of representational control required to build such freedom was astonishing. For instance, the wall has three steel "windows" in it. There are 52 working drawing sheets for the windows alone.

The wall is constructed from one thousand 8" x 8" x 8" concrete blocks, each block specially cut. My office produced the steel shop drawings for a pipe structure that supports the blocks (no steel fabricators were willing to be responsible). Another thirty two sheets.

There are also my drawings, models, computer models, drawings on models, drawings on drawings – an enormous graphic package that confirms the freedom/control paradox.

Again, the subject is the drawn representation and technical control required to build a design conception that is about the opposite.

So, is conceptual freedom architectural freedom? Or do the demands for the drawn representation of architecture negate the freedom concept?

```
try {

    int i;
    for( int j=0; j<h; j++){
      for(int k=0; k<3; k++){
        for( i=0; i<w; i++){

          int red   = (pixels[j*w+i] [illegible]
          int green = (pixels[ [illegible]
          int blue  = (pixels [illegible]

            if(i==0)file.writeBytes("\n");
            if(k==0 && red>99)file.writeBytes("" + red);
            if(k==0 && red<10)file.writeBytes("00" + red);
            if(k==0 && red<100 && red>9)file.writeBytes("0" + red);

            if(k==1 && green > 99)file.writeBytes("" + green);
            if(k==1 && green<10)file.writeBytes("00" + green);
            if(k==1 && green<100 && green>9)file.writeBytes("0" + green);

            if(k==2 && blue > 99)file.writeBytes("" + blue);
            if(k==2 && blue<10)file.writeBytes("00" + blue);
            if(k==2 && blue<100 && blue>9)file.writeBytes("0" + blue);
          }
      }
    }
  }
```

Prix.Swiczinsky.Himmelb(l)au.
COOP HIMMELB(L)AU

The Architecture of Clouds

There is no solution for the city.

The strategies of urban planning operate on the matrix of diverging impossibilities.

The architect has to choose one and claim responsibility for it.

Clouds are symbols for conditions that change quickly. They form and transform themselves through the complex interaction of changing situations. Viewed in slow motion, the architecture of urban development could be compared with patches of clouds.

The vocabulary of urban planning should be in an architectural antique shop and replaced by phantasms still to be defined, which fluctuate and flicker like the television screen after broadcast.

The white noise of urban strategy, a digitally networked system without hierarchy, is the play of suburb and periphery which will mold and determine the image of our cities and the quality they have to offer.

The notions of center, axis and spatial sequence will have to be replaced by tangent, vector and sequence of images. We should not regret the loss of public space, but reinterpret it as a fluctuating, networked media event. One which acts more like a semi-conductor than a sequence of spaces.

The development of architecture is also furthered by strategies which are compromised by searching for lines and fields of possibilities tied together by chance, anti-logic and anti-authority.

The coincidence of systems – both as built space and as media space – becomes the basis for new designs and projects; the rubber-grid as the premonition of a dynamic design-net for cities like clouds.

010
014
015

Andrea Zittel and Jonathan Williams

A-Z Pocket Property Prototypes

The collaborative image of Micro Space/Global Time created by Andrea Zittel and Jonathan Williams, illustrates a prototype for A-Z Pocket Property, a project which will be realized over the next three years in the Öresund, a body of waters between Sweden and Denmark.

A-Z Pocket Property is conceived as a piece of land, a habitat, and a vehicle all combined into a compact and consumable package. The "product" in this case will function both as Zittel's own experimental living situation, and as a critique on the way in which our culture constructs and then capitalizes on a human desire for freedom, autonomy, and isolation. The A-Z Pocket Property will be built by layering concrete over a hollow armature, creating a structure which literally enables the owner to live "inside" of their own "land". Similar to a series of identical plots that compose a suburban neighborhood, the Pocket Property can be mass produced, and the identical units can be customized to meet individual needs. The outer surface of the land formation is designed to be landscaped in such a way as to suggest a variety of different terrains: the inside can be modified into a unique and personalized living space.

The image created for Micro Space/Global Time is the first collaboration between Zittel and Williams. Working from one of Zittel's plaster models of the island, Williams created a three-dimensional image of the form using Alias/Wavefront software and mapped one of his landscape paintings to the surface as a texture. Together, Zittel and Williams developed the selection of images for the print.

The final renderings of the A-Z Pocket Property are not intended to function as a schematic; rather they are more a means for the artists to project themselves psychologically into the scenario of living on one's own private island. To imagine what elements would become necessities, and what it would feel like to be alone in the middle of a vast ocean, was an exercise in projecting oneself into a digitally constructed environment.

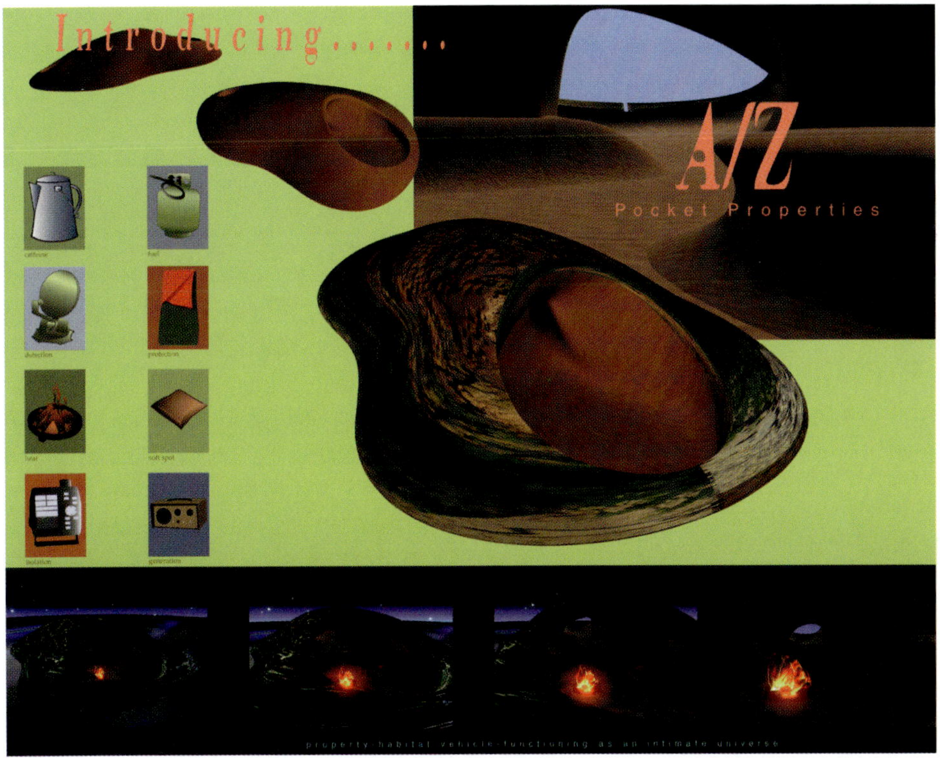
Introducing.......
A/Z
Pocket Properties
fuel
detection
protection
heat
soft spot
isolation
generation
property habitat vehicle functioning as an intimate universe

Biographies

Vito Acconci
Acconci Studio, New York

Vito Acconci's work began as fiction and poetry in which the page was treated as a self-enclosed space for writer and reader to travel through. His first work in an art context, in the late 60s and early 70s, took the form of events and performances, film and video, which functioned as instruments of self-exploration and person-to-person relationships. In the mid-70s, his audio and video installations were designed for specific exhibition spaces which were used as community meeting-places. The participatory sculpture of the early 80s involved the viewer in the raising and razing of structures which in turn raised and razed the power-signs of a culture. In the mid-80s the work focused on architecture, landscape-architecture and furniture design. Since the late 80s, he has worked with a group of architects as Acconci Studio; together, they have proposed and built projects for public places – streets and plazas, gardens and parks, building lobbies and transportation centers. An indoor park for the Philadelphia Airport has recently been completed: soon to be completed are a seating system for the 161st Street Subway station in the Bronx, New York and a movable landscape for the Buildings Department Administration Building in Munich.

Neil M. Denari
Neil M. Denari Architects, Los Angeles

Founded in 1988, Neil M. Denari Architects work on a broad range of scale using state of the art computer software to design and render space. The firm has produced competitions, projects, installations and writings addressing issues of technology and contemporary culture. In 1997, Neil Denari was appointed Director of the Southern California Institute of Architecture (SCI-Arc). Recent and upcoming publications include *Interrupted Projections* (Toto Inc., 1996) which explores the contemporary landscape of advertising, media saturation and the poetics of technology in our time and *Gyroscopic Horizons* (Princeton Architectural Press and Thames and Hudson) currently in production.

Craig Hodgetts and Hsin-Ming Fung
Hodgetts + Fung Design Associates, Los Angeles

Craig Hodgetts is an architect and urban scenarist known for his imaginative adaptation of architectural form to the challenges of cultural change, urban evolution and developing technology. Hsin-Ming Fung

is an architect, educator and director of Hodgetts + Fung Design Associates. Her practice is informed by her unique cultural perspective and by a belief in the vitality of urban forms as the generator of human occasion.
Joining forces in 1984 to form Hodgetts + Fung Design Associates, the two have worked on the historic renovation and adaptive reuse of the Egyptian Theater in Hollywood, the redesign and update of the Hollywood Bowl and a new studio building for Otis College of Art and Design.

Greg Lynn
FORM, Los Angeles

Greg Lynn opened his architectural office, FORM, in 1994. Current projects on which he is collaborating with other young architects include the Hydrogen House for the OMV Corporation in Vienna – a prototype house and visitors' center for a large oil refinery. Mechanical and electrical systems for these buildings are powered by a combination of passive and active solar systems and a hydrogen gas fuel cell like that used for the American space program. Another project is the Korean Presbyterian Church of New York, a 3,000' addition to an existing factory in New York City. In addition to his practice, he teaches throughout the U.S. and Europe. Recent publications include *Animate: FORM* (Princeton Architectural Press, 1999) and *Folds, Bodies and Blobs: Collected Essays* (La Lettre Volée, 1998).

Thom Mayne
Morphosis, Los Angeles

Thom Mayne founded Morphosis in 1972 under the premise that design is a collective enterprise. The design objective focuses on the multiple needs predicated by the project brief, site and client. Morphosis has been the recipient of 20 Progressive Architecture awards, 28 AIA awards as well as numerous other design recognitions. Their work is published extensively in prominent architecture publications around the world incuding two upcoming monographs: *Morphosis Buildings and Projects 1993-1997* (Rizzoli, 1999) and *Morphosis* (C3 Publications, 1999). One of the founding members of the Southern California Institute of Architecture, Mayne continues to serve on the board of directors while also holding a faculty position at UCLA School of Art and Architecture.

Eric Owen Moss
Eric Owen Moss Architects, Los Angeles

Founding his office in Los Angeles in 1973, Eric Owen Moss has created award-winning projects around the world and is responsible for the on-going revitalization and redesign of Culver City, an industrial area of Los Angeles. His work has been featured in numerous exhibitions and in 1996 he was selected as one of four American architects to represent the U.S.A. at the Venice Biennale. Recently he received the 1999 Award in Architecture from the American Academy of Arts and Letters. His recent and upcoming publications include: *Eric Owen Moss: Buildings and Projects 2* (Rizzoli, 1995); *The Box* (Princeton Architectural Press, 1996); *The Lawson/Westen House* (Phaidon Press, 1994); *Gnostic Architecture* (Monacelli Press, 1998); *PS and 10 Years and the New City* (Images Press, 1998); *Buildings and Projects 3* (Rizzoli, 2000)

Wolf D. Prix, Helmut Swiczinsky
COOP HIMMELB(L)AU, Vienna

COOP HIMMELB(L)AU was founded in 1968 in Vienna, Austria by Wolf D. Prix and Helmut Swiczinsky and continues to work in the fields of architecture, design and art. COOP HIMMELB(L)AU has realized projects which range from remodelings in Vienna to city planning projects in France. The most recognized projects are the Rooftop Remodeling in Vienna, Austria; the masterplan for the city of Melun-Sénart in France; and the Museum Pavilion in Groningen, Netherlands. Wolf D. Prix is professor of the Masterclass of Architecture at the University of Applied Arts in Vienna.

Andrea Zittel and Jonathan Williams, Los Angeles

Andrea Zittel is an artist currently living and working in Los Angeles. She received her MFA from the Rhode Island School of Design in 1990 and has exhibited widely across the U.S. and in Europe including exhibitions such as documenta X and Sculpture Projects in Münster. Known for her sculptural installations, Zittel creates designs for living which explore how the structures used in daily life signify values, beliefs and desires. Her recent work addresses issues connected to the human construction of terrain and territory under the rubrick, A-Z Land Brands. Jonathan Williams is a painter also living and working in Los Angeles. Williams uses digital media to distance his work from the painterly gesture and to find meaning in shape, line and color. His paintings employ both traditional and computer-generated figuration.

Exhibition Checklist

Vito Acconci
World in your Bones, 1999
Iris print on watercolor paper
33" x 45" (page 13)

Neil Denari
Untitled, 1999
Crystal Archive type C print
33" x 45" (page 15)

Craig Hodgetts and Hsin-Ming Fung
RE.T.V., 1999
Iris print on watercolor paper
45" x 33" (page 17)

Greg Lynn
Embryological Space, 1999
Iris print on watercolor paper
33" x 45" (page 19)

Thom Mayne
Untitled, 1999
Crystal Archive type C print
33" x 45" (page 21)

Eric Owen Moss
Untitled, 1999
Iris print on watercolor paper
45" x 33" (page 23)

Prix.Swiczinsky.Himmelb(l)au
The Architecture of Clouds, 1999
Crystal Archive type C print
33" x 45" (page 25)

Andrea Zittel and Jonathan Williams
A-Z Pocket Property Prototypes, 1999
Crystal Archive type C print
33" x 45" (page 27)

All prints published in an edition of 20 with additional 10 artist proofs.

ISBN 0-9671862-1-8